Move Ahead

Grammar Practice Book 2

EDWARD WOODS

CONTENTS

Note

The exercises in this Grammar Practice Book generally follow the sequence of the Grammar Reference section at the end of Move Ahead Student's Book 2. The focus here is mainly on form, but students also have the chance to think, as well as to know. The table of contents gives a detailed summary of the grammatical focus in each exercise and, in some cases, of the type of language practice asked for.

PAGE

1 Put the verbs in the brackets in the verb forms indicated.

1 They _____ to Scotland in September for a holiday.

(*often go*, present perfect)

2 Mary _____ anything from that new shop.   (*never buy*, future)

3 She _____ the owners charge too much.   (*think*, present simple)

4 That film _____ by more than two million people in one week.

(*see*, past simple passive)

5 When he _____, he _____ more than $2000 a

week.   (*work*, past continuous; *earn*, past simple)

6 The soldiers _____ prisoner, if they _____ that

town.   (*take*, future simple passive; *enter*, present simple)

7 A large area of Sydney _____ by the bush fires.

(*destroy*, past simple passive)

8 At the moment, Bob _____ for the government.

(*still work*, present continuous)

9 Jane _____ here any longer.   (*not live*, present simple)

10 That painting _____ by the greatest French artist of the

nineteenth century.   (*do*, past simple passive)

2 Make the following sentences negative.

1 Tom will visit his aunt next Sunday.

_____

2 They played tennis yesterday.

_____

3 I watched TV last night.

_____

4 We are learning English at school.

_____

5 Meg likes to go to the theatre.

_____

6 I was given this ring by my mother.

_____

7 Elizabeth has bought a new car.

_____

8 Terry and Bill work in Germany.

_____

9 They have been cooking burgers.

_____

10 Ivan has been to London this year.

_____

3 Now make the sentences in Exercise 2 into questions.

1 _____

2 _____

3 _____

4 _____

5 _____

6 _____

7 _____

8 _____

9 _____

10 _____

4 Read the manager's speech to the football club. Put the verbs in brackets into the correct forms.

Ladies and gentlemen:

This (**1** *be*) _____ a great day for our football team. This year, we

(**2** *come*) _____ first in our group, and today we (**3** *win*) _____

a great victory by eight goals to one.   Our team (**4** *play*) _____ well all

this season, but today our players (**5** *play*) _____ very well.

What (**6** *do*) _____ they _____ now? They (**7** *enjoy*) _____

_____ a big party.

Last year, we (**8** *come*) _____ near the bottom of our group. We

(**9** *play*) _____ very badly. How (**10** *change*) _____ we

_____ all that?

Last summer we (**11** *work*) _____ very hard.   The players (**12** *train*)

_____ every day. When the season (**13** *begin*) _____, they

(**14** *be*) _____ very fit.

How (**15** *play*) _____ they _____ next season? We must

wait and see.

5 **Read about holiday travel. Put the verbs in brackets into the correct forms.**

These days, many people in northern countries (**1** *travel*) _____ long

distances for their holidays. Often, people from the same country (**2** *go*) _____

to the same place, for example, lots of English people (**3** *enjoy*) _____

going to Spain and lots of Swedes (**4** *fly*) _____ to The Gambia in Africa.

Why? They (**5** *look*) _____ for the sun.

　　What (**6** *do*) _____ they _____ many years ago? In Britain

people (**7** *go*) _____ to the seaside. Sometimes they (**8** *find*) _____

the sun. In Sweden, they (**9** *go*) _____ to the countryside. But since the

1960s, people (**10** *travel*) _____ to the hot, southern countries.

6 **Read this holiday postcard. Put the verbs in brackets into the correct forms.**

We (**1** *have*) _____ a lovely holiday. Tim (**2** *make*)

_____ friends with a boy who lives here. Now they (**3** *go*)

_____ surfing together every day. Martin and I (**4** *go*)

_____ to the beach every morning. Yesterday we (**5** *see*)

_____ a huge fish. Martin (**6** *say*) _____ it (**7** *be*)

_____ a shark – like Jaws! But I (**8** *not believe*)

_____ him and (**9** *laugh*) _____. In the afternoon,

we (**10** *go*) _____ on a tour of the island. We (**11** *walk*)

_____ to some interesting caves in the hills and we (**12** *see*)

_____ some very old drawings on the walls. Martin and I (**13**

come) _____ home at the end of the month. We (**14** *not be*)

_____ sure about Tim. His new friend (**15** *invite*)

_____ him to stay for another week.　　　　Jenny

2 DIRECT AND INDIRECT OBJECTS

1 Put the words in brackets in the correct order in the sentence. Do not add any extra words.

1 I'll pay _____ next week. (*him, his salary*)

2 They showed _____. (*their holiday photographs, them*)

3 I sent _____ to the party. (*an invitation, her*)

4 They didn't tell _____. (*the whole truth, the police*)

5 I wrote _____, but he didn't answer any of them. (*him, three letters*)

6 Give _____ on the table, please. (*the book, me*)

7 Could you lend _____? (*four pounds, me*)

8 He bought _____ for her birthday. (*her, some flowers*)

9 They promised _____, if he finished the job by the end of the month. (*Tim, a lot of money*)

10 You owe _____, and I need it now! (*£3,000, me*)

2 Put the words in brackets in the correct order.

1 Jane gave _____. (*it, him*)

2 They took _____. (*presents, John*)

3 Peter showed _____. (*the picture, him*)

4 Ben offered _____ (*a ticket, Ray*), but he didn't offer _____. (*Bob, one*)

5 We owe _____. (*you, some money*)

6 Tell _____. (*your story, them*)

7 Mr Darling lent _____. (*the book, to his son*)

8 At bedtime, his mother always read _____. (*a story, the boy*)

9 Please pass _____. (*the coffee, Miss Brown*)

10 Pay _____! (*the money, the man*)

3 Make the sentences passive, using the underlined words as the subject.

1 They offered <u>Dalia</u> the manager's job.

_____

2 His wife told Alan <u>the sad story</u>.

_____

3 They bought the best seats in the stadium for <u>the guest</u>.

_____

4 She showed <u>him</u> her new painting.

_____

5 They awarded Mary <u>the prize</u>.

_____

6 They promised <u>Derek</u> a share of the prize money.

_____

7 They bought the old lady <u>some chocolates</u>.

_____

8 They offered David <u>one of the new computers</u>.

_____

9 They told <u>the prisoner</u> his punishment.

_____

10 They sent <u>Mr Brown</u> an invitation.

_____

4 Rewrite the following sentences in the active form.

1 Mr Roberts was given £1000, when he left his job.

_____

2 I was offered the job by the manager.

_____

3 Hannah was shown the new car by her husband.

_____

4 Daisy Miller was awarded the prize for being the best student of the year.

_____

5 Richard was told everything about the accident.

_____

6 He was owed a lot of money by his cousin.

_____

7 She was lent the book.

_____

8 He was paid his salary at the end of the month.

_____

9 He was promised a place in the football team.

_____

10 When she was a child, she was always read a story at bedtime.

_____

1 **Make the following noun structures plural.**

1 bottle of milk _____   2 milk bottle _____

3 loaf of bread _____   4 bread pudding _____

5 electricity bill _____   6 garden gate _____

7 kitchen door _____   8 shop assistant _____

9 football crowd _____ 10 box of sweets _____

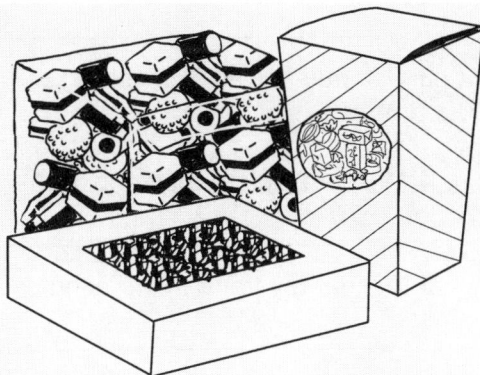

2 **Match the words in column A with those in column B. Where there are two possibilities, write both.**

EXAMPLE: **A**   **B**

cows   herd   *herd of cows*

water   bottle   *water bottle, bottle of water*

A	B	
toothpaste	flock	_____
road	tube	_____
crowd	bar	_____
flowers	game	_____
chocolate	people	_____
cake	accident	_____
birds	bunch	_____
bread	bottle	_____
lemonade	slice	_____
chess	piece	_____

3 Explain the meaning of the following noun structures.

EXAMPLE: The washing machine safety instructions

The instructions for safely using the machine for washing (clothes).

1 The swimming pool entrance gate

_____

2 The jewellery box key

_____

3 Computer sales success

_____

4 Museum picture theft shock

_____

5 The railway travel information centre

_____

_____

_____

_____

4 Put the these words in the correct column below.

advice	furniture	work	hope	car	bank	language	news
film	sugar	canal	money	group	day	wood	electricity
night	year	ball	ink	fruit	paper	office	bread	chocolate
history	van	information	water	love			

Uncountable		Countable		Both
_____	_____	_____	_____	_____
_____	_____	_____	_____	_____
_____	_____	_____	_____	_____
_____	_____	_____	_____	_____
_____	_____	_____	_____	_____
_____	_____	_____	_____	_____

5 **Correct these sentences, if necessary. Tick the sentence if it is already correct.**

1 There were no furnitures in the room. _____

2 He gave me good advice. _____

3 Finally there were some good news. _____

4 He has no hope for the future. _____

5 I don't take a sugar in my coffee. _____

6 Have you any informations about that? _____

7 The water is very cold. _____

8 There's a bread in the box. _____

9 There were no inks in the shop. _____

10 Put the milks in the fridge. _____

6 **Fill in the correct form for the noun in brackets. If the noun is countable, use the plural form. If it is uncountable, do not use the plural form.**

The school physics and chemistry (**1** *laboratory*) _____ needed some

new (**2** *equipment*) _____. New (**3** *furniture*) _____ was

also needed. The (**4** *staff*) _____ got (**5** *information*)

_____ and placed (**6** *order*) _____ with the education

(**7** *supplier*) _____. When everything arrived, the (**8** *technician*)

_____ wanted to do some (**9** *experiment*) _____. The

head teacher gave some (**10** *advice*) _____ on what to do. He was

very pleased with their (**11** *work*) _____.

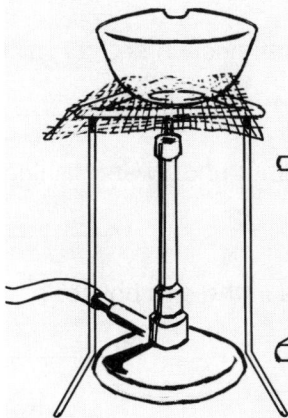
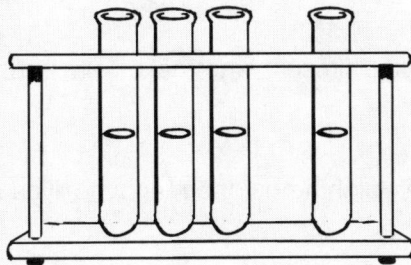
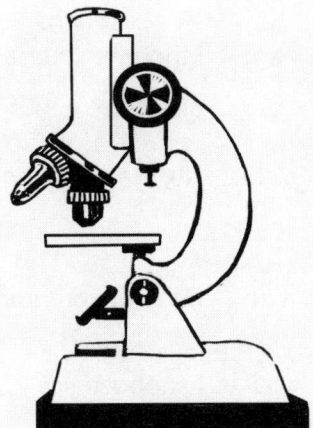

1 **Decide which of the relative clauses in the dialogue are defining and which are non-defining.**

EXAMPLE: Ann and Meg, who are best friends, are talking together.   *non-defining*

Ann is asking about the neighbour who makes films.   *defining*

ANN: Do you know the man who lives in the end house?   **(1)** _____

MIRIAM: Do you mean the big house which faces the river?   **(2)** _____

ANN: Yes. Do you know the man who lives there?   **(3)** _____

MIRIAM: No. Why should I?

ANN: I thought you would. He's a very rich man, who makes films.

(4) _____

MIRIAM: Why should I know a man who makes films?   **(5)** _____

ANN: I thought your father was a cameraman, who sometimes worked for this film

director.   **(6)** _____

MIRIAM: No. He's a film maker himself, who makes films about underwater fishing.

(7) _____

ANN: Oh. But your father might know the man who lives in the end house.

(8) _____

MIRIAM: I suppose so.

2 Study the table below and then answer the questions. In each answer, you should add a relative clause saying something about the person. Show whether the relative clause is defining or non-defining by correct use of punctuation. Look carefully at the example answers.

Name	House number	Sport	Favourite animal	Friend
Mustapha	16	running	elephant	Anna
The man	23	football	dog	Ali
The woman	8	tennis	cat	Miriam
Miriam	15	swimming	monkey	the woman
Anna	32	basketball	zebra	Mustapha
Ali	6	sailing	snake	the man

EXAMPLES: Who lives at number 16?   *Mustapha, who likes running*

Who lives at number 8?   *The woman who likes cats*

1 Who lives at number 23? _____

2 Who plays basketball? _____

3 Who likes cats? _____

4 Who likes snakes? _____

5 Who is the swimmer? _____

6 Who is Mustapha's friend? _____

7 Who plays tennis? _____

8 Who lives at number 6? _____

9 Who is Miriam's friend? _____

10 Who likes elephants? _____

3 Below is a description of Lancaster, which is an old town in northern England. The description can be improved by inserting the relative clauses in the box into the correct sentences. You must decide whether to introduce the clause with *who* or *which*. When you have decided which clause to insert, make sure you put commas around the non-defining clauses.

> *is for less dangerous criminals   is also the Duke of Lancaster*
> *have lived there   gets its name from the river Lune   is a very old city*
> *has had many famous prisoners   is twenty miles away*
> *has always been a prison   is an important tourist area*

Lancaster (**1**) lies in the north-west of England.

The Queen (**2**) owns a lot of property in the area.

On the hill, there is an old castle (**3**).

The prison (**4**) is the oldest working prison in Britain.

It is a grade C prison (**5**).

Lancaster (**6**) was once the capital city of a large area

called Lancashire. Nowadays the capital is Preston (**7**).

From the castle, you can see the mountains of the Lake District (**8**).

The Lake District is famous for many writers and artists (**9**).

_____

_____

_____

_____

_____

_____

_____

1 Complete the table by writing the past simple tense and the past participle. The first one has been done for you.

Verb	Past simple	Past participle	Verb	Past simple	Past participle
1 begin	_began_	_begun_	**12** have	_____	_____
2 bend	_____	_____	**13** hear	_____	_____
3 bring	_____	_____	**14** know	_____	_____
4 catch	_____	_____	**15** read	_____	_____
5 come	_____	_____	**16** run	_____	_____
6 do	_____	_____	**17** say	_____	_____
7 drink	_____	_____	**18** see	_____	_____
8 drive	_____	_____	**19** sing	_____	_____
9 eat	_____	_____	**20** take	_____	_____
10 give	_____	_____	**21** wear	_____	_____
11 grow	_____	_____	**22** write	_____	_____

2 Write the correct tense of the verb – past simple or present perfect. Use the present perfect wherever possible.

EXAMPLE: He (*do*) _has done_ the homework.

He (*do*) ____did____ the homework last night.

1 Mary (*get*) _____ the tickets yesterday.

2 Robert (*teach*) _____ English in Turkey last month.

3 Sally (*pass*) _____ all her exams.

4 Professor Large (*be*) _____ head of department for three years.

5 David (*paint*) _____ a lot of pictures last year.

6 He (*win*) _____ the top prize in December.

7 I (*see*) _____ the latest Star Wars film.

8 Anne (*visit*) _____ Australia many times.

9 They (*buy*) _____ a new car last week.

10 Many forests near Sydney (*burn*) _____ down in 2002.

17

3 Write the replies to these questions.

EXAMPLE: Has Brian run in the London Marathon race?

No, he *hasn't* , but his brother *ran* in it last month.

1 ANN: Have you been to Rome?

BEN: Yes, I _____ . I _____ there in May.

2 TIM: Did you see the Eiffel Tower when you were in Paris?

JOE: No, I _____ , but I _____ it many times before.

3 GRANDMA: Has John finished his exams yet?

MOTHER: Yes, he _____ . He _____ them last week.

4 MAX: How long have you lived here?

JOHN: I _____ here since 1995. Before that, I _____
in Berlin.

5 TOM: Did Uncle Pat have a holiday last year?

FATHER: No, he _____ . In fact, he _____ a holiday
for ten years.

6 BILL: Did you see that film on TV last night?

ANDY: No, of course, I _____ . I (*sell*) _____ my TV!

7 MARY: Have you bought a new car?

SUE: Yes, I _____ . I _____ it a month ago.

8 FATHER: Have you sent that letter to the tax office?

MOTHER: Yes, I _____ . I _____ it last week.

9 FATHER: Did Richard visit Grandpa last week?

MOTHER: No, he _____ . But he _____ him this week.

10 AMY: Did you go to the computer class yesterday?

ROSE: No, I _____ . I _____ not _____ for a long time.

4 Choose the correct tense for the verbs in brackets. Use the past simple or the present perfect.

In 2001, many parts of Great Britain (**1** *suffer*) _____ badly because of a disease which affects cows and sheep. Even now, the tourist industry (**2** *not recover*) _____ properly. I (**3** *visit*) _____ many of the areas. In April, I (**4** go) _____ to Cumbria in the north-west, which (**5** *be*) _____ one of the worst-hit areas. Many hotels (**6** *have to*) _____ close because tourists (**7** *have to*) _____ stay away from these areas in 2001. The owners (**8** *lose*) _____ all their money. The outbreak (**9** *make*) _____ people think about farming methods in Great Britain. In the past, the farmers (**10** *take*) _____ their animals long distances to be killed. This (**11** *cause*) _____ the disease to spread rapidly. Now they (**12** *decide*) _____ that the whole industry must be reorganised.

5 Complete the sentences by putting the verbs in the present perfect continuous.

1 He (*work*) _____ on that project for two years, and it's still not finished.

2 She (*learn*) _____ English for three years, but she can't speak it very well.

3 Let me drive. You (*drive*) _____ for the last 150 kilometres.

4 The speaker (*talk*) _____ for two hours. I wish he'd stop. It's very boring.

5 The forest fires (*burn*) _____ for three weeks now. We need a lot of rain to put them out.

19

6 Complete the dialogue by putting the verbs in the present perfect or the present perfect continuous.

TOM: Hello, Peter. I (**1** *not see*) _____ you for ages. What

(**2** *do*) _____ you _____ ?

PETER: I (**3** *work*) _____ for a film company. It's very

interesting.

TOM: (**4** *make*) _____ you _____ any films?

PETER: Yes. I (**5** *make*) _____ two films about south-east

Asia. For the last two months, I (**6** *work*) _____ on a

film about the islands in the Pacific.

TOM: (**7** *go*) _____ you _____ to the islands?

PETER: Of course. And the film will be about the underwater life around the islands.

So I (**8** *have*) _____ diving lessons. I (**9** *enjoy*)

_____ that.

TOM: You (**10** *find*) _____ a really interesting job!

1  **2**  **3**  **4**  **5**

6  **7**  **8**  **9**

1 Write statements about the pictures above like one of the examples below.

EXAMPLES: *They should get the windows cleaned.* or *They must get the windows cleaned.*

1 _____

2 _____

3 _____

4 _____

5 _____

6 _____

7 _____

8 _____

9 _____

2 Look at the pictures in Exercise 1 again and write statements like the example.

EXAMPLE: <u>*They had the windows cleaned*</u> by The Window Company.

1 _____ by Joseph's Hair Styles.

2 _____ by Robinson's TV Repairs.

3 _____ by City Car Service.

4 _____ by the gardener.

5 _____ by John Budd House Painter.

6 _____ by Hunt's House Service.

7 _____ by the High Street Garage.

8 _____ by the dry cleaners.

9 _____ by the plumber.

3 Rewrite the sentences below in the imperative form.

EXAMPLES: The windows need cleaning.   ~~Get the windows cleaned.~~

They need to clean the windows.   ~~Get the windows cleaned.~~

I want the windows cleaned.   ~~Get the windows cleaned.~~

1 That operation needs doing. _____

2 That shirt needs repairing. _____

3 Those tests need marking. _____

4 They need to sell that house. _____

5 They need to cut the tree down. _____

6 I want the snow cleared. _____

7 I need to fit new windows. _____

8 I want to have my dinner cooked. _____

9 The guest-room needs tidying. _____

10 He needs to upgrade his computer. _____

4 **Put the correct preposition after the adjective.**

1 There's nothing to be afraid _____ .

2 Are you interested _____ seeing that film?

3 I was very disappointed _____ his work.

4 They were amazed _____ his skill.

5 The boss was very satisfied _____ the clerk's work.

6 I'm tired _____ waiting for him.   He's always late.

7 They were worried _____ his remarks.

8 She was frightened _____ strangers.

9 They were very involved _____ the new business.

10 I was surprised _____ his rudeness.

1 Match the sentences on the left with those on the right. Write the letter of the matching sentence in each box.

1 Have you heard the weather forecast? ☐	**a** He's going into hospital today.
2 Those rocks are dangerous. ☐	**b** I'm going to see the films.
3 I liked the Harry Potter books. ☐	**c** It'll make a lot of money.
4 What are your plans for the holiday? ☐	**d** It's going to snow.
5 The traffic is very bad today. ☐	**e** I'm going to hear it on Friday.
6 Grandpa was very ill last week. ☐	**f** I'm going to travel to China.
7 Jane isn't going to school this week. ☐	**g** Careful! You'll fall.
8 It's Mary's birthday on Saturday. ☐	**h** There'll be an accident soon.
9 The film's very popular. ☐	**i** She'll be eighty-five years old.
10 There's a very good concert next week. ☐	**j** Her cold may get worse.

2 Complete the sentences by putting the verb in brackets in the correct tense. Use either the present simple or the present continuous.

1 The train _____ at 7 o'clock. (*arrive*)

2 John _____ to dinner tonight. (*come*)

3 _____ you _____ the holiday with Dick? (*spend*)

4 The tour of the castle _____ at midday. (*begin*)

5 The flight to Budapest from London _____ two hours. (*take*)

6 The bus _____ at four-thirty. (*leave*)

7 I _____ the new teacher on Friday. (*meet*)

8 The school holidays _____ on 7th July. (*start*)

9 Usually, we _____ back to school at the end of August. (*go*)

10 Mary _____ to her new house next Tuesday. (*move*)

SPEEDY MOVE COMPANY

3 Join the clauses using one of the subordinating conjunctions below. Use each conjunction only once.   Put the verbs in brackets in the correct tense.

> *although   as soon as   because   before   if   since*
> *so that   when   where   while*

EXAMPLE: They'll go. They (*be*) ready.

They'll go when they are ready.

1 We'll start. John (*arrive*).

_____

2 Will he know? They (*live*).

_____

3 I'll tell him. I (*see*) him.

_____

4 We'll work all day. We (*finish*) the job tonight.

_____

5 They bought the book. It (*be*) very expensive.

_____

6 You'll be there by one o'clock. You (*take*) the early train.

_____

7 They'll pay him a lot of money. He always (*do*) a good job.

_____

8 I haven't seen him. He (*return*) from his trip.

_____

9 Ben won't be able to get to the cinema. The film (*start*).

_____

10 What will you do? He (*be*) on holiday.

_____

4 Put the verbs in brackets in the correct tense for the function given in the box.

ADAM: What (**1** do) _____ at the weekend? `fixed arrangement`

BILL: I (**2** go) _____ to the beach. Do you want to come?

`fixed arrangement`

ADAM: I can't. I (**3** have) _____ a picnic. `intention`

BILL: Oh!

ADAM: All my friends (**4** come) _____ . (**5** be able) _____

_____ to come? `4 fixed arrangement; 5 general`

BILL: I'd like to, but I (**6** go) _____ to the beach with Mary and

Jack. `fixed arrangement`

ADAM: Mary and Jack? Are you sure? They (**7** come) _____ to

my picnic. They've already told me. `prediction with evidence`

BILL: What time (**8** be) _____ your party? `timetable`

ADAM: Four o'clock in the afternoon.

BILL: It (**9** be) _____ a nice day on Saturday according to the

weather forecast. But I (**10** come) _____ to the party,

when I get back from the beach. `9 prediction with evidence; 10 promise`

ADAM: (**11** bring) _____ Mary and Jack with you? `request`

BILL: Of course. I (**12** let) _____ you know the time as soon as

I've spoken to them `promise`

ADAM: All right. Thanks. 'Bye.

1 Join the pairs of sentences by using *and*, *but* or *so*. In some sentences, more than one conjunction is possible. Write other possible conjunctions in brackets.

EXAMPLES: Joe was ill on Monday. He couldn't do the exam.

Joe was ill on Monday and (so) he couldn't do the exam.

We searched everywhere. We still couldn't find it.

We searched everywhere but (and) we still couldn't find it.

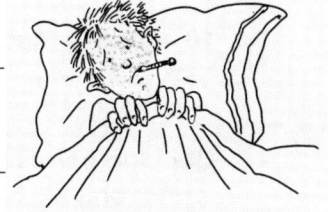

1 She worked very hard. She passed the exam.

_____

2 It was a bad accident. No-one was seriously hurt.

_____

3 They've got a very big house. They've got a very expensive car.

_____

4 The television broke yesterday. Now the radio doesn't work.

_____

5 I couldn't go to the theatre. I gave the tickets to John.

_____

6 He was the best applicant. He got the job.

_____

7 Rob was very tired. He continued to work.

_____

8 There's no bus after 10 pm. You'll have to walk home now.

_____

9 They don't let you in after the play begins. You must get there on time.

_____

10 All the baggage had come off the plane. John's suitcase wasn't there.

_____

2 Join the pairs of sentences by using _either ... or, both ... and,_ or _not only ... but._

1 He passed the exam. He got the best grades.

_____

2 Alice and Jane went to Canada for their holiday. They took a cruise.

_____

3 The man looked after the garden. He also kept the house tidy.

_____

4 John was very tall. He was very strong.

_____

5 She could spend the money on a car. She could buy a small apartment.

_____

6 Spain has a very warm climate. It has some very good beaches.

_____

7 In their business, they built houses. They designed bridges.

_____

8 Robert went camping with Leo. In the winter, he went climbing with him.

_____

9 King John lost the battle. He also lost all the jewels.

_____

10 Mozart was a great composer. He was a great piano player.

_____

3 Underline the main clause in the following sentences.

1 Although the computer was very small, it was very expensive.

2 The police got to the scene of the crime as soon as they could.

3 When they got there, the thieves had disappeared.

4 The houses were built by the park, even though building wasn't allowed there.

5 Budapest is a city where there are many fine buildings.

6 You will only see a shortened version of the film if you watch it on TV.

7 The government will lose the election if they don't solve the crisis.

8 The colour of the universe was blue when there were a lot of young stars.

9 The family will sell the business as soon as their father dies.

10 The Queen was popular because she did her job well.

4 Complete the text below with the following conjunctions.

alternatively   furthermore   however   moreover   otherwise   so   therefore

Rome is one of the most fascinating of Italy's historic cities. (**1**) _____,
there is more to see here than any other city in the world. (**2**) _____, in
terms of modern culture, it is not like a capital city. You can, (**3**) _____,
visit some classical buildings thousand of years old. (**4**) _____, you can
wander down narrow alleys and streets of a much later time. Rome has typical
features of many different historic periods. You shouldn't, (**5**) _____,
expect to see everything on your first visit. (**6**) _____ plan to see only a
few places, (**7**) _____ you will get very tired. (**8**) _____, you
will always want to come back again and again.

29

9 THIRD-TYPE CONDITIONALS AND PERFECT MODALS

1 Match the sentence beginnings on the left with suitable endings on the right.
Write the letter of the correct ending in each box.

1 Napoleon might have got to Moscow ☐   **a** if I had worked harder.

2 We would have arrived sooner ☐   **b** if it had been cheaper.

3 She would have bought the dress ☐   **c** if she had been cleverer.

4 They wouldn't have lost the game ☐   **d** if the weather had been better.

5 The thief wouldn't have got into the house ☐   **e** if he had been more careful.

6 I might have got the job ☐   **f** if their best player hadn't been ill.

7 He wouldn't have fallen ☐   **g** if they hadn't gone to Italy again.

8 I could have cooked the dinner ☐   **h** if they had locked all the doors.

9 He might have married her ☐   **i** if the car hadn't broken down.

10 I would have gone with them ☐   **j** if you had asked me.

2 Rewrite each sentence below as a third-type conditional using the modal verb in brackets.

EXAMPLE: He didn't get home early because the train was delayed. (*would*)

He would have got home early if the train hadn't been delayed.

1 I didn't buy the chair because it was too expensive. (*would*)

_____

2 He didn't finish the work because he was too tired. (*might*)

_____

3 She didn't come because she didn't like Meg's friend. (*might*)

_____

4 They couldn't go on holiday because he had lost the plane tickets. (*would*)

_____

5 They couldn't go out because they hadn't finished their work. (*could*)

_____

6 He didn't like the hotel because the rooms were too small. (*would*)

_____

7 I was only able to do it because he helped me. (*could*)

_____

8 I didn't do it because you didn't ask me. (*would*)

_____

9 They didn't arrive earlier because there was a bad road accident. (*might*)

_____

10 The police couldn't arrest the suspect because he had left the country. (*could*)

_____

3 **Put the sentences in the past.**

EXAMPLE: I must leave early.   *I should have left early.*

1 I must talk to her about the holiday.

_____

2 Joe should not spend so much time watching TV.

_____

3 They will finish the work by Wednesday.

_____

4 The fires may be started deliberately.

_____

5 It can't be true that nobody saw the attack.

_____

6 They would tell him about the accident.

_____

7 Jane is very clever and could be head of the company.

_____

8 The clown could make the children laugh.

_____

9 They wouldn't buy their daughter the game because it was too expensive.

_____

10 Could he be the man who won the tennis championship?

_____

4 **Complete the sentences below by using the perfect modals of *must* or *can't*.**

1 Surely he (*finish*) _____ already! He's only been working on it for half an hour.

2 Surely he (*finish*) _____ by now! He's been working on it for hours.

3 You (*see*) _____ Jane in town yesterday. She's on holiday in Greece.

4 Peter (*write*) _____ that letter. He's the only person who knew about your aunt.

5 Daisy (*buy*) _____ that car. She doesn't have the money. Her father (*buy*) _____ it for her.

6 The thieves (*get in*) _____ through the small window. It was left open by accident.

7 You (*see*) _____ that film already. It only started yesterday.

8 You (*get*) _____ the job. They wouldn't be sending you all that information if you hadn't got it.

9 I don't believe Jack. He (*get*) _____ the highest grades in the exam. He never does any work.

10 He (*write*) _____ that essay. He (*get*) _____ _____ his friend to help him.

1 **Put the verbs in brackets in the correct tense.**

1 I wish they (*sign*) _____ the treaty soon, but I know they won't.

2 I wish I (*buy*) _____ that coat, but I didn't.

3 They wish they (*live*) _____ near the sea, but they don't.

4 Her husband wishes she (*not argue*) _____ so much, but she does.

5 She wishes he (*make up*) _____ his mind, but he won't.

6 The student wishes he (*have*) _____ passed the exam, but he didn't.

7 I wish the rain (*stop*) _____ by now, but it hasn't.

8 The local people wish the shop (*not close*), _____ but it has.

9 I wish I (*can*) _____ paint, but I can't.

10 They wish they (*not forget*) _____ the party, but they did.

2 **Put the verbs in brackets in the correct tense.**

SAM: I wish I (**1** *know*) _____ about the concert Mary gave last week.

ADAM: Why?

SAM: Well, I wish I (**2** *see*) _____ her playing. Everyone says she's a wonderful musician.

ADAM: She certainly is. I wish I (**3** *can*) _____ play the violin as well as she can. I used to play when I was younger, but I gave it up. Now, of course, I wish I (**4** *not stop*) _____ playing. Have you really never heard Mary play the violin?

SAM: No, I haven't. I wish I (**5** *hear*) _____ her. I have always planned to go to one of her concerts, but I have never had the time yet.

ADAM: That's a pity! I really wish you (**6** *go*) _____ to hear her last week because she's decided not to give any more concerts. She's going to concentrate on teaching younger players.

SAM: Oh, no! I didn't know that! I wish she (**7** *give*) _____ just one more concert.

ADAM: Perhaps we can persuade her.

SAM: Do you think so? Well, I wish you (**8** *ask*) _____ her. She likes you. Tell her it's just for her friends.

ADAM: All right. I'll say that we all wish she (**9** *make*) _____ a final, final appearance. Wish me luck!

1 Use the correct infinitive or –ing form of the verb in brackets in the following sentences.

1 They agreed _____ the explorer the money. (*give*)

2 He hoped _____ the Antarctic. (*cross*)

3 His first task involved _____ the right people for the team. (*find*)

4 Those people risked _____ their lives in the extreme cold. (*lose*)

5 The footballer promised _____ properly in the future. (*behave*)

6 He gave up _____ into the city centre after the match. (*go*)

7 He admitted _____ involved in an argument at a restaurant. (*be*)

8 He hoped _____ for his club for many years. (*play*)

9 Florence Nightingale didn't enjoy _____ as an idle, rich lady. (*live*)

10 She wanted _____ something useful in her life. (*do*)

2 **Complete the sentences.**

EXAMPLE: *'Please go!'* I asked him ___*to go*___ .

1 *'Don't do it!'* I told them _____ .

2 *'Where can I go?'* He doesn't know _____ .

3 *'I'd like to help you.'* I've come here _____ .

4 *'Come with us to the theatre.'* We invited her _____ .

5 *'Who can help me?'* I'm looking for someone _____ .

6 *'I don't know who wrote "Romeo and Juliet".'* The schoolboy wanted

_____ _____ .

7 *'Please stay a bit longer.'* We begged them _____ .

8 *'How can I do it?'* He didn't know _____ .

9 *'Everything's paid for.'* There's nothing _____ .

10 *'I'm going to sell my product overseas.'* The factory owner decided _____

_____ .

3 **Make the underlined section the subject of the sentence.**

EXAMPLE: It should be easy to open this box.

Opening this box should be easy.

1 It isn't hard to find work here.

_____

2 It should be interesting to hear what he has to say.

_____

3 It must be difficult to live with him.

_____

4 It's fun to work in a record shop.

_____

5 It's relaxing for Jim to do the housework.

_____

6 It will be very expensive to go to the Caribbean for a holiday.

_____

7 It can be dangerous <u>to ski off the proper routes.</u>

_____

8 It would be polite <u>to tell him we can't go on Tuesday.</u>

_____

9 It might be a bad idea <u>not to invite them.</u>

_____

10 It was strange <u>to meet him in that restaurant.</u>

_____

4 **Put the verbs in brackets in the correct infinitive or *-ing* form.**

After (**1** *spend*) _____ the evening with a group of the villagers in a small village in Japan, David Preston was invited (**2** *join*) _____ them for a game of cards. They all went across to the fire station. While (**3** *look*) _____ at the fire engine, David asked one of the men (**4** *explain*) _____ what all the parts were for. (**5** *see*) _____ that the different parts interested David, the man suggested (**6** *go*) _____ out for a ride. The other men quickly agreed (**7** *go*) _____ with them and soon they were driving around the village (**8** *sound*) _____ the siren and (**9** *wake*) _____ all the villagers. They rode around the village three or four times, when they were suddenly stopped by a policeman. After (**10** *talk*) _____ to them, he took them to the police station.

1 Match these questions with the reported questions below. Write the number of the question in the correct box.

1 (Is Joe coming home next week?) **2** (Will Mary be here tomorrow?)

3 (When is there going to be an announcement?) **4** (Have you bought a new car, Tom?)

5 (Did you like that film on TV?) **6** (Where are you going to spend your holiday?)

7 (Do you like learning English?) **8** (How high is Mount Everest?)

9 (How much did that watch cost?) **10** (How is your family?)

a Elizabeth asked if he had liked the film on TV. ☐

b She asked Tom if he had bought a new car. ☐

c They wanted know how much the watch had cost. ☐

d He enquired if Joe was coming home the following week. ☐

e His friend asked Ned if he liked learning English. ☐

f They asked how the family was. ☐

g The teacher wanted to know if Mary would be there the next day. ☐

h Mary asked Jack where he was going to spend his holiday. ☐

i The teacher asked the pupils how high Mount Everest was. ☐

j The journalist wanted to know when there was going to be an announcement. ☐

2 Write down what changes were made in the reported questions.

is changed to _____   *you* changed to _____

have changed to _____   *tomorrow* changed to _____

am coming changed to _____

3 Read through this interview in a police station between Detective Inspector Bell and Jim James, a suspect in a bank robbery, then do the tasks that follow.

D.I. BELL: Why were you at the bank, Mr James?

JIM JAMES: Pardon?

D.I. BELL: I asked you why you were at the bank.

JIM JAMES: To get some money, of course.

D.I. BELL: Was it your money?

JIM JAMES: Er… I don't understand.

D.I. BELL: I was enquiring if it was your money.

JIM JAMES: Oh, yes, of course it was.

D.I. BELL: Have you always had an account there?

JIM JAMES: I'm sorry, I didn't hear that.

D.I. BELL: I wanted to know if you had always had an account there.

JIM JAMES: Why do you want to know?

D.I. BELL: I'm asking the questions, Mr James, so don't ask me why I want to know. Tell me. Have you always had an account there?

JIM JAMES: No.

D.I. BELL: So why did you go there?

JIM JAMES: I don't have to answer that.

D.I. BELL: I think you do. Now then, I asked you why you went there.

JIM JAMES: I needed some money. That was the nearest bank. OK?

D.I. BELL: Well, that's all for the moment. I'll speak to you again later.

1 Underline all the reported questions.
2 Write down what changes were made in the reported questions.
3 Were they the same changes that you noticed in Exercise 1?
4 What were the differences?

4 Write the reported question.

1 (What's your name?)

David asked the new customer _____.

2 (Are you going to marry Tom?)

Alice asked me _____.

3 (Where have you been?)

The mother asked her son _____.

4 (Has Ali already left for his holiday in France?)

Tim enquired _____ .

5 (Will you be able to pay back the money tomorrow?)

He asked if _____.

6 (Who is the best football player in the country?)

The boys wanted to know _____.

7 (How much do you need to buy that car?)

I asked you _____.

8 (How far is the sun from the Earth?)

The examiner asked her _____.

9 (How do you cook couscous?)

I asked you _____.

10 (Do I have to finish this work by Saturday?)

The builder wanted to know _____.

5 **Write the original question.**

1 The reporter wanted to know how long the emergency would last.

_____

2 The actor asked me if he had got a part in the play next week.

_____

3 The writer wanted to know how the dinosaurs had become extinct.

_____

4 Mary enquired how long it would take to go from London to Istanbul by train.

_____

5 They asked people if it was better to eat fish rather than meat.

_____

6 They wanted to know why the bus had broken down last week.

_____

7 They wanted to know what the distance was between the Great Lakes of North America and the Gulf of Mexico.

_____

_____

8 The philosopher wanted to know what the meaning of life was.

_____

9 The scientist asked you if you knew what asteroids were.

_____

10 He asked the zookeeper where grass snakes lived.

_____

6 Below is part of an interview with a young film actor, Mat Fraser. Write the questions and answers in a reported form.

FILM Review

Star News
Win a DVD player

Mat Fraser interview

INTERVIEWER: What is your idea of perfect happiness?

1 The interviewer asked Mat _____

MAT: It's spending a day off with my parents and my two brothers.

2 Mat replied _____

INTERVIEWER: What is your greatest fear?

3 The interviewer wanted to know _____

MAT: It's forgetting my lines when the cameras are running.

4 Mat answered _____

INTERVIEWER: Who do you most admire?

5 The interviewer asked Mat _____

MAT: My father, who is always patient and understanding.

6 Mat said _____

INTERVIEWER: What do you hope to do in the future?

7 The interviewer wanted to know_____

MAT: I'd like to try directing one day.

8 Mat told him _____

INTERVIEWER: What is your advice to other young people who want to be actors?

9 The interviewer asked him _____

MAT: My advice is to finish your school studies before you start acting – I'm

              very glad I did!

10 Mat said _____

1 Rewrite the sentences below with the adverb in brackets in the correct place.

1 Richard has visited Budapest. (*often*)

_____

2 He gets excited when he is there. (*very*)

_____

3 He stays with a friend. (*in the centre of the city*)

_____

4 He likes to walk everywhere in the city. (*surprisingly*)

_____

5 He visits the galleries and museums. (*at the weekends*)

_____

6 He goes to a concert. (**a** *usually*; **b** *on Thursdays*)

_____

7 He meets many old friends. (*there*)

_____

8 He likes to arrive. (*early*)

_____

9 After a concert, he goes to a restaurant. (*sometimes*)

_____

10 He enjoys having a meal with some good friends. (*very*)

_____

2 Look again at Exercise 1 and say what type of adverb is in each sentence.
Choose one of these: degree, frequency, manner, place, sentence adverb, time.

1 _____	2 _____	3 _____	4 _____
5 _____	6a _____	6b _____	7 _____
8 _____	9 _____	10 _____	

3 Read these sentences. Tick (✔) the five which are correct. Cross (✗) and rewrite correctly the five which are wrong.

1 I haven't got enough money to go to the cinema. ☐

2 He didn't work enough hard to pass the exam. ☐

3 Is it warm for you enough in this room? ☐

4 There aren't enough chairs for everyone here. ☐

5 He didn't arrive enough early to see the parade. ☐

6 They couldn't find players to make enough a team. ☐

7 I haven't enough time to do all that. ☐

8 She didn't swim enough fast to break the record. ☐

9 The teacher didn't have enough books for all the class. ☐

10 Is the bus early enough for us to get to the cinema on time? ☐

_____

_____

_____

_____

_____

4 Complete the dialogue with *too*, *very*, or *enough*.

FATHER: We need to buy a new car.

MOTHER: It's (**1**) _____ expensive.

FATHER: But it's (**2**) _____ important for my job.

MOTHER: We don't have (**3**) _____ money. What's wrong with the old one?

FATHER: It's old, and there's not (**4**) _____ room for my work things.

MOTHER: You don't use it (**5**) _____ much for work.

FATHER: I would use it more if it was big (**6**) _____ .

MOTHER: But I need it for the shopping! There's often (**7**) _____ much to carry.

FATHER: Perhaps we need two cars then.

MOTHER: That's (**8**) _____ silly.

FATHER: So what shall we do?

MOTHER: You do the shopping.

5 Complete these sentences with an appropriate adverb of the type shown in brackets.

EXAMPLE: _Sometimes_ , the weather is in the news around the world. (*frequency*)

1 _____ there were a lot of strange events. (*time*)

2 For example, it rained heavily _____ . (*place*)

3 _____ , it was very hot in October in Britain. (*sentence adverb*)

4 A _____ strange insect was found in the Pacific. (*degree*)

5 There were _____ epidemics around the world. (*frequency*)

6 Newspapers reported these events _____ . (*manner*)

7 It is now _____ easy to fly cheaply in Europe. (*degree*)

8 Many cheap airlines go to the biggest cities _____ . (*frequency*)

9 Take Prague. You can now fly _____ for just £20. (*place*)

10 _____ , I don't have enough money just now. (*sentence adverb*)

6 Complete the text by underlining the best adverb of the type given in brackets.

The Royal Mail Coach is the name of a (**1** *degree*) **really** / **often** / **fortunately** popular restaurant in Budapest. We went (**2** *place*) **quickly** / **outside** / **there** / one evening. My friend (**3** *frequency*) **too** / **always** / **never** / goes there because he enjoys the live jazz music. However, I found it was (**4** *degree*) **unfortunately** / **never** / **very** / loud. (**5** *sentence adverb*) **Luckily** / **Slowly** / **Usually**, I liked the restaurant. They cooked the food (**6** *manner*) **quietly** / **well** / **sometimes** and served (**7** *degree*) **here** / **extremely** / **rarely** large helpings.

45

1 Read this information.

Adjectives can describe: **a** what something is made of
b its colour
c its purpose
d its size
e where it comes from

2 Study these phrases and write what each adjective describes as listed in Exercise 1.

EXAMPLE: the blue hat _colour_   the blue sun hat _colour, purpose_

1 the brown bag _____   **2** the brown paper bag _____

3 the big ball _____   **4** the big beach ball _____

5 the red vase _____   **6** the red Italian vase _____

7 the Turkish bowl _____

8 the Turkish glass bowl _____

9 the small green coffee cup _____

10 the small green china coffee cup _____

_____

3 Arrange the list in Exercise 1 correctly to show the order of adjectives going before a noun.

1 _____

2 _____

3 _____

4 _____

5 _____

4 Put the adjectives in brackets in the most suitable order before the nouns.

1 _____ car (*green, sports, French*)

2 _____ computer (*brown, British, small*)

3 _____ train (*long, black and red, London*)

4 _____ boat (*fishing, blue, big, wooden*)

5 _____ house (*wooden, family, black*)

6 _____ man (*Australian, white, tall*)

7 _____ chair (*brown, office, leather, Italian*)

8 _____ book (*exercise, green, thin*)

9 _____ table (*dining, Swedish, large, glass*)

10 _____ box (*Indian, small, wooden, jewellery, red*)

5 Rewrite the following sentences putting all the adjectives before the noun.

EXAMPLE: The office building was tall and made of concrete.

It was a tall, concrete, office building.

1 The bridge was long and made of steel.

_____

2 The clock was Spanish and made of china.

_____

3 The plates were white and large, were used for soup and made in France.

_____

4 The hunting dog was big and brown.

_____

5 The racing horse was tall and white and came from Morocco.

_____

6 The leather box was very small and came from Turkey.

_____

6 Complete this story by writing the adjectives in brackets in the correct order.

THE FISHING CLUB ROBBERY

'Being a senior member of the fishing club is a big responsibility, Inspector.' Ali

insisted as he looked across the (**1** *oak, office, big*) _____

desk. 'When I came in, I was shocked to find the place in such a mess. Those (**2** *iron,*

black, Swedish) _____ chairs were just thrown around.

Those (**3** *wooden, desk, small*) _____ drawers were on

the floor and the (**4** *membership, blue*) _____ forms were scattered everywhere. I saw immediately that the (**5** *iron, small*) _____

safe in the corner was open and the money gone.'

'You've tidied this room up very quickly, sir.'

'There was nothing else to do while I waited for you.'

'A pity. You may have destroyed evidence.'

'I never thought of that.'

'Where were you, sir, before you got here?'

'I went fishing.'

'At sea? It was a very rough day.'

'I know. I was pleased to get back safely. The (**6** *black, huge*) _____

waves crashed over my (**7** *fishing, big, Egyptian*) _____ boat.'

'When did you get back, sir?'

'About half an hour ago. Of course, I phoned you immediately.'

'Before you tidied up.'

'Yes. I said I did that while waiting for you.'

The inspector looked at Ali in his (**8** *black, fishing, leather*) _____

clothes. The clothes were dry. 'You've no idea who would take the money?' He leant

back in the (**9** *green, large, desk*) _____ chair.

'Of course not.'

'I think you do. We will have to discuss this at the police station.'

7 Complete the sentences by putting the correct preposition after the adjectives.

1 Joan is afraid _____ snakes.

2 John's mother was very proud _____ him after he passed the exam.

3 Manchester is famous _____ football.

4 Mike was very interested _____ the history of Egypt.

5 Greta was very kind _____ Josie when she was ill.

6 He lost his job because he was always late _____ work.

7 At school, I was very bad _____ Maths.

8 Television has too many game shows. I'm very bored _____ them now.

9 The football team was ashamed _____ the fans after the riots.

10 After a week without any news, the people became very worried _____ the men on the Antarctic expedition.

1 Underline the correct preposition in the sentences below.

1 He should be here **by** / **during** eight o'clock.

2 David and Victoria have been married **for** / **since** / **until** 1998.

3 The war continued **for** / **since** / **during** five years.

4 I won't be home **until** / **since** Monday.

5 They promised to finish the work **until** / **by** the weekend.

6 I lived in Rome **since** / **for** two years.

7 He'll finish the work, even if he has to do it **during** / **by** his holiday.

8 He's had that car now **since** / **for** 1999.

9 She's going away **since** / **for** three months.

10 He was president **during** / **by** a very difficult period for his country.

2 Complete the dialogue with the correct prepositions.

ANDREW: Hello, Bob. I haven't seen you (**1**) _____ a long time.

BOB: No. I've been working abroad. I went to Germany two years ago and was

there (**2**) _____ last month.

ANDREW: So you were there (**3**) _____ the election period.

BOB: Yes. It was very interesting. I had a friend who worked for one of the political

parties. He had to work every night (**4**) _____ May.

ANDREW: They have elections every four years. Can they hold them any time

(**5**) _____ the four years?

BOB: Yes. But usually they don't. Here in Britain, it's different.

ANDREW: We can have an election any time. Even six months after the last one.

BOB: Yes, but we must have one at least every five years. So we must have our next election (**6**) _____ the end of next year.

ANDREW: That's right. And the politicians will wait (**7**) _____ the last minute before they tell us. Are you going back to Germany?

BOB: I'd like to, but I must do some work here (**8**) _____ the next two years.

ANDREW: In this town?

BOB: No, I'll only be here (**9**) _____ Sunday. I've got to go up north. I've been here (**10**) _____ the beginning of the month doing nothing. Now I want something to do. It's been good meeting you. 'Bye.

ANDREW: 'Bye. Have a good time in the north.

3 **Complete the paragraph by putting in the correct prepositions. As you read, imagine yourself as the puddle, a small pool of water left after rain has fallen.**

THE STORY OF A PUDDLE

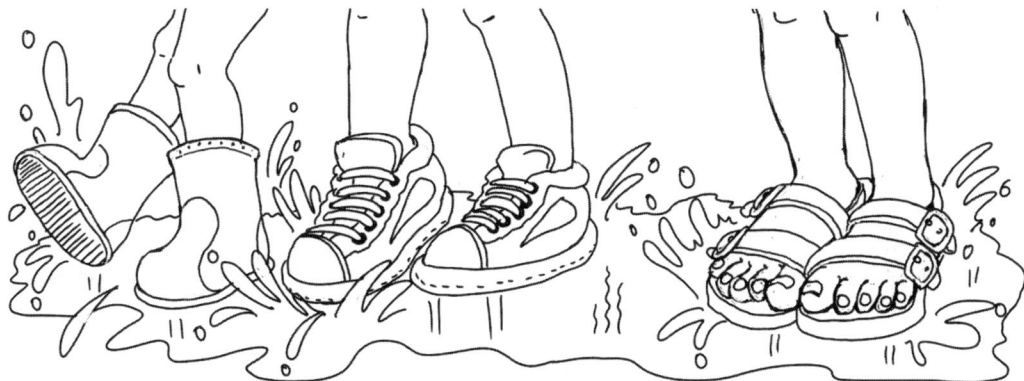

I have been in this street (**1**) _____ early this morning. In fact, I've been here (**2**) _____ hours. I don't often stay this long, but this morning it has been very cloudy and damp. (**3**) _____ the morning, many children have walked through, splashing me everywhere. I've lost a lot of water. Now the sun is coming out. If it gets very hot, I shall start to dry up and I shall be gone (**4**) _____ three o'clock this afternoon. It's going to rain again tonight. (**5**) _____ the night, new puddles will form, so that (**6**) _____ morning, there will be a lot of water for the children to splash about.

(from an idea by *Istvan Orkeny*, 1912-1979) **51**

16 POSITION OF PREPOSITIONS

1 **Put the words in the following sentences in the correct order.**

1 were speaking you to who? _____

2 to someone to he talk wants. _____

3 house of we're looking sort the for that's. _____

4 are for what you that doing? _____

5 paid car the now for is. _____

6 story written the down has been. _____

7 are at laughing you what? _____

8 she's tree down had the cut. _____

9 with Ben needs someone play to. _____

10 I him man that's the with saw. _____

2 **Say which of the following structures each sentence in Exercise 1 is:**
wh-question; relative clause; passive clause; causative; infinitive clause.

1 _____   **2** _____

3 _____   **4** _____

5 _____   **6** _____

7 _____   **8** _____

9 _____   **10** _____

3 **Rewrite the dialogue putting in one of these prepositions wherever possible.**

> *about   after   around   at   by   for   from   in   on   to   with*

ANN: Did you see the play television last night?

MARY: No. What time was it?

ANN: Eight o'clock.

MARY: I was busy then. An old friend school called.

ANN: Oh! You must have had a lot to talk.

MARY: We did. She's been working Australia.

ANN: I've always wanted to go Australia. Where was she?

MARY: First she was Sydney, then she went Melbourne.

52   ANN: I've got an aunt Sydney. Did she like Australia?

MARY: Oh, yes. She stayed ten months, March December.

ANN: How wonderful. There are so many interesting places to go.

MARY: Yes, she left Melbourne, she travelled the country.

ANN: Did she go train or bus?

MARY: Both, I think.

ANN: Did she travel anyone?

MARY: Yes, she went a friend. Anyway, what was the play like?

ANN: Oh, I didn't see it. I wanted to know if you did. Then you could have told me it.

ANN: _____

MARY: _____

ANN: _____

MARY: _____

ANN: _____

MARY: _____

ANN: _____

MARY: _____

ANN: _____

MARY: _____

ANN: _____

MARY: _____

ANN: _____

MARY: _____

ANN: _____

MARY: _____

ANN: _____

MARY: _____

1 Put the words in the sentences below in the correct order. Where there are two possibilities, write both.

1 do yourself it you did?

_____

2 grass herself the she cut.

_____

3 themselves they concert organised the.

_____

4 himself house the he let into.

_____

5 to she talking herself was.

_____

6 house built they themselves the.

_____

7 fighting were among they themselves.

_____

8 her himself he hated hurting for.

_____

9 work must we do ourselves the.

_____

10 I myself that do could.

_____

2 Now look again at Exercise 1 and decide whether each pronoun is reflexive or emphatic.

1 _____ 2 _____ 3 _____

4 _____ 5 _____ 6 _____

7 _____ 8 _____ 9 _____

10 _____

3 In this dialogue, the reflexive and emphatic pronouns have been left out. Complete it with the appropriate pronoun then say whether each is emphatic or reflexive.

ALISON: That's a lovely painting. Did you do it (**1**) _____?

PAULINE: Of course. I work by (**2**) _____. There's nobody else.

ALISON: I didn't know you could paint so well. I (**3**) _____ am quite useless.

PAULINE: You can't be. Nobody is. Try again. I've always told (**4**) _____ that if I really wanted to do something, then I could do it.

ALISON: Perhaps you're right.

PAULINE: Of course I am! Look, I remember your flat when you moved in. It was in a terrible condition. You decorated it (**5**) _____ and now it looks lovely.

ALISON: Well, I had to do it (**6**) _____, because I had nobody to help me! Anyway, I must think about going home now. Oh dear!

PAULINE: What's wrong?

ALISON: I've forgotten my keys. I've locked (**7**) _____ out!

PAULINE: Not again! You must remind (**8**) _____ to pick them up before you go out.

ALISON: I could write (**9**) _____ a big note and put it on the front door.

PAULINE: That's a good idea, but remember to read it!

1 _____ 2 _____ 3 _____

4 _____ 5 _____ 6 _____

7 _____ 8 _____ 9 _____

Macmillan Education
Between Towns Road, Oxford OX4 3PP
A division of Macmillan Publishers Limited
Companies and representatives throughout the world

ISBN 0 333 78907 5

Text © Edward Woods
Design and illustration © Macmillan Publishers Limited 2002

First published 2002

Designed by Ann Samuel
Illustrated by Sarah Wimperis, Graham Cameron Illustration
Cover design by Wheeler and Porter
Cover photo by Alamy

Printed and Bound by Zamzam Presses, Egypt

2006 2005 2004 2003
10 9 8 7 6 5 4 3 2